Eckels

# Fun with Paragraph Writing

Author ................ Linda Milliken
Illustrator ............. Barb Lorseyedi
Editor ................. Kathy Rogers

**Reproducible for classroom use only.**
**Not for use by an entire school or school system.**
EP164 • ©2002 Edupress, Inc.™ • P.O. Box 883 • Dana Point, CA 92629
www.edupressinc.com
ISBN 1-56472-164-7
Printed in USA

# Table of Contents

**Page**

### People & Communities
- 3   Related Studies and Activities
- 4   City Life
- 5   Farm Life
- 6   Neighborhoods
- 7   School Days
- 8   Sports
- 9   Community Helpers
- 10   Careers
- 11   The Carnival
- 12   Gardens
- 13   Trees

### Communication, Travel & Government
- 14   Related Studies and Activities
- 15   Newspapers
- 16   Elections
- 17   Presidents
- 18   Liberty Bell
- 19   Stars & Stripes
- 20   Transportation
- 21   Summer Vacation

### Understanding Others
- 22   Related Studies and Activities
- 23   Family Life
- 24   Mother
- 25   Father
- 26   Friends
- 27   Disabilities

### History
- 28   Related Studies and Activities
- 29   Kings & Queens
- 30   Castles & Knights
- 31   Ancient Egypt
- 32   Native American Legends

**Page**

- 33   Explorers
- 34   Coming to a New Land
- 35   Pioneers
- 36   Cowboys
- 37   Martin Luther King, Jr.
- 38   African Americans

### Countries & Cultures
- 39   Related Studies and Activities
- 40   Travel
- 41   Foreign Food
- 42   United States
- 43   Canada
- 44   Eskimos
- 45   Africa
- 46   Mexico
- 47   Japan

### Seasons, Holidays & Traditions
- 48   Related Studies and Activities
- 49   Snow!
- 50   Fall Fun
- 51   Birthdays!
- 52   Presents
- 53   Pumpkins
- 54   Ghost Story
- 55   Turkey and Trimmings
- 56   Hanukkah
- 57   Christmas Traditions
- 58   Santa Claus
- 59   Reindeer
- 60   Chinese New Year
- 61   Groundhog Day
- 62   My Valentine
- 63   Leprechauns
- 64   Bunnies

# People & Communities
## Related Studies and Activities

Encourage students to explore individual topics on their own, using the related studies and suggested activities listed below.

**City Life**
**Related Studies:** Ethnicity • Family Roots • Immigrants • Towns
**Activity:** Write a short story about a family member who grew up in the city. Attach a photo.

**Farm Life**
**Related Studies:** Farm Animals • Harvesting • Milk Production
**Activity:** Create a sequential, timed schedule of a day's chores on a farm.

**Neighborhoods**
**Related Studies:** Neighbors • Apartment Houses • Country Living
**Activity:** Make a cooperative photo album of your neighborhood.

**School Days**
**Related Studies:** Teachers • Principals • Education • Learning Disabilities
**Activity:** Draw a map of your school grounds.

**Sports**
**Related Studies:** Teamwork • Football • Baseball • Soccer • Gymnastics
**Activity:** Write a news report about a sporting event you saw on television or in person.

**Community Helpers**
**Related Studies:** Fire • Hospitals • Libraries & Librarians • Volunteers
**Activity:** Make a chart of community helpers and write a summary about the job each of them does.

**Careers**
**Related Studies:** Education • Earning Money • Planning for the Future
**Activity:** Dress up for a classroom career day and present a short talk about the career you represent.

**The Carnival**
**Related Studies:** Fairs • Parades • Animals • Lifestyles
**Activity:** Plan and participate in a classroom or school carnival.

**Gardens**
**Related Studies:** Flowers • Soil • Earthworms • Compost • Vegetables
**Activity:** Divide into groups and assign each group a flower or vegetable to plant, raise, and report on.

**Trees**
**Related Studies:** Arbor Day • Fruit • Gardening • Leaves • Paper Making
**Activity:** Take a "tree hike" and keep track of how many different kinds of trees are observed.

# City Life

What does a city sound like? Are the sounds you hear in a city different than those you would hear in the country?

| Close your eyes and imagine you are in the city during the daytime. Make a list of sounds you might hear. | Close your eyes and imagine you are in the city during the nighttime. Make a list of sounds you might hear. |
|---|---|
| | |

Select one of your word lists and write a paragraph describing a daytime or nighttime adventure in the city.

_____
_____
_____
_____
_____
_____
_____
_____

*Fun with Paragraph Writing*

# FARM LIFE

Would you like to live on a farm? There are a lot of interesting things to see and do, but there is also a lot of hard work!

Pretend you are a farmer.
Make a list of your chores for the day.

**Things to Do:**

1. _____
2. _____
3. _____
4. _____
5. _____

Make a list of animals that you would have on your farm.

**Farm Animals:**

1. _____
2. _____
3. _____
4. _____
5. _____

Now write a brief letter to a friend describing your day working on the farm!

_____
_____
_____
_____
_____
_____
_____
_____

Pretend you are a reporter for your local newspaper. Your assignment is to write an article about something that happened in your neighborhood.

Begin by writing two or three ideas for each section of the house. Then select your best idea and write at least two paragraphs of a newspaper article. Use the back of the page or another sheet of paper for your article.

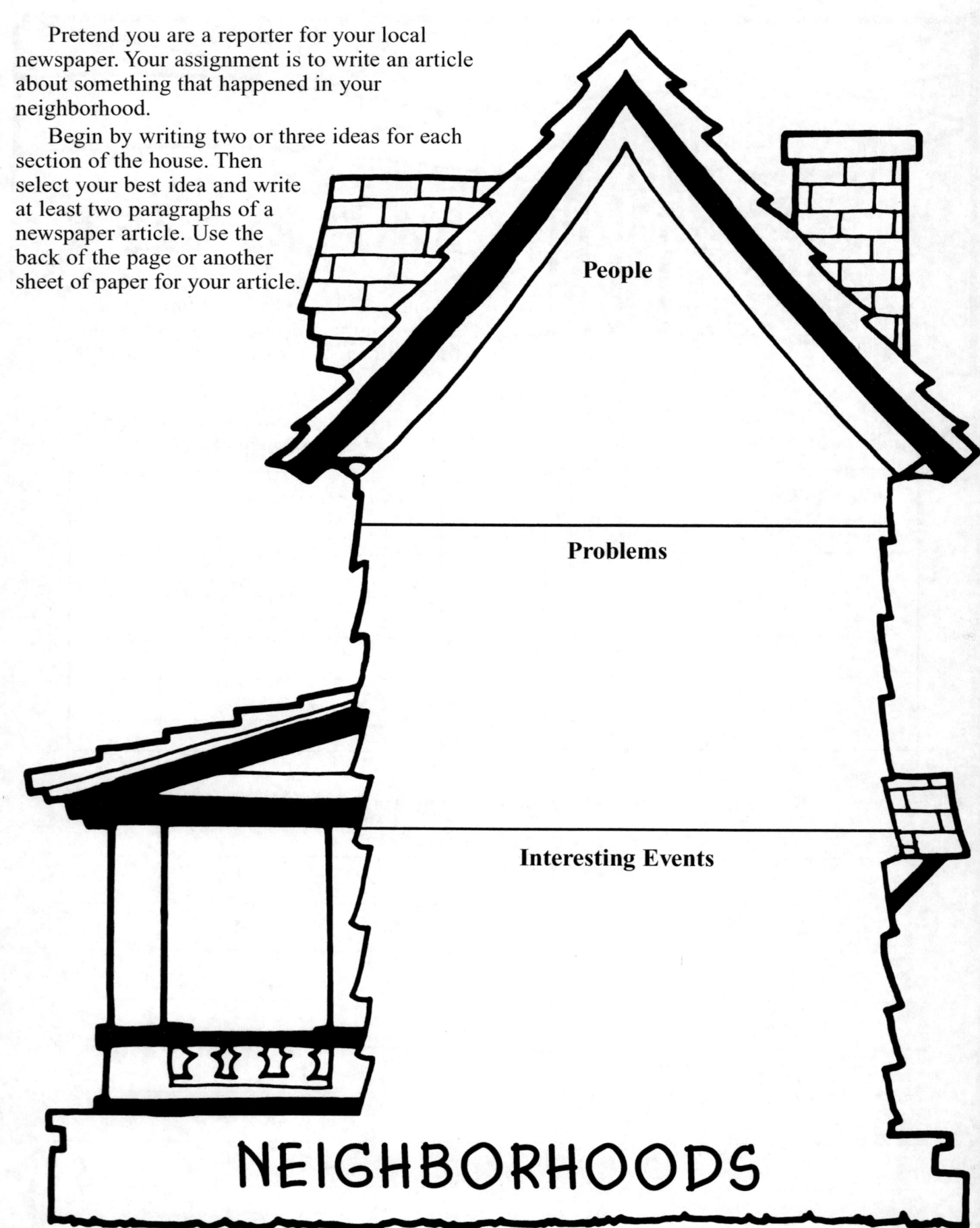

**People**

**Problems**

**Interesting Events**

# NEIGHBORHOODS

# School Days

1. In the first box, write a paragraph describing a perfect day at school.
2. Give your paper to a friend and have him or her read it, then write any corrections and comments in the second box.
3. Read your friend's corrections and comments. Decide what changes you think should be made, and write your paragraph again in the third box.
4. Read your final paragraph out loud to the class.

*Fun with Paragraph Writing*

© EDUPRESS, INC.™   EP164

# SPORTS

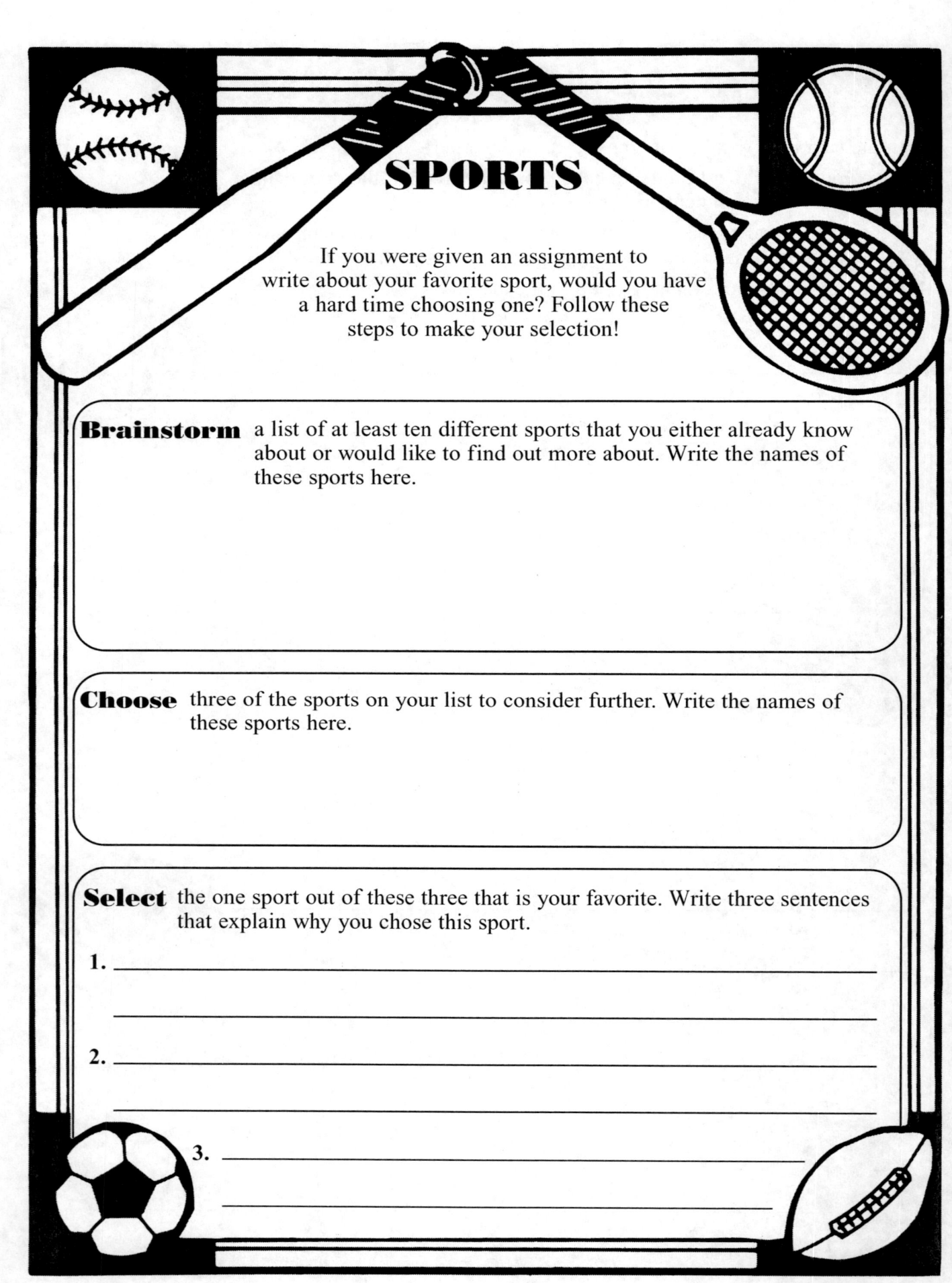

If you were given an assignment to write about your favorite sport, would you have a hard time choosing one? Follow these steps to make your selection!

**Brainstorm** a list of at least ten different sports that you either already know about or would like to find out more about. Write the names of these sports here.

**Choose** three of the sports on your list to consider further. Write the names of these sports here.

**Select** the one sport out of these three that is your favorite. Write three sentences that explain why you chose this sport.

1. _____

2. _____

3. _____

# Community  Helpers

There are many community helpers whom we rely upon: firefighters, police officers, mail carriers, librarians, and teachers, for example. Select one of these helpers or another one of your choice and think about the work that they do.

Write three questions you would ask to learn about this person's job.

1. _____
2. _____
3. _____

Use the space below to write a description of your community helper's job. Write at least four sentences, and add as many interesting details as you can think of.

_____
_____
_____
_____
_____
_____
_____
_____

*Fun with Paragraph Writing* © EDUPRESS, INC.™ EP164

# Careers

Carpenter, barber, doctor, dentist. Do any of these careers sound interesting to you?

In each of the blocks below, write a list of five words that tell about what a person in that career does. Then write a sentence in each box describing that career, using at least one of the words on your list. Then turn your paper over and write a paragraph explaining which of the careers you would choose and why.

### Carpenter

1. ____________________
2. ____________________
3. ____________________
4. ____________________
5. ____________________

________________________________________

________________________________________

### Barber

1. ____________________
2. ____________________
3. ____________________
4. ____________________
5. ____________________

________________________________________

________________________________________

### Dentist

1. ____________________
2. ____________________
3. ____________________
4. ____________________
5. ____________________

________________________________________

________________________________________

### Doctor

1. ____________________
2. ____________________
3. ____________________
4. ____________________
5. ____________________

________________________________________

________________________________________

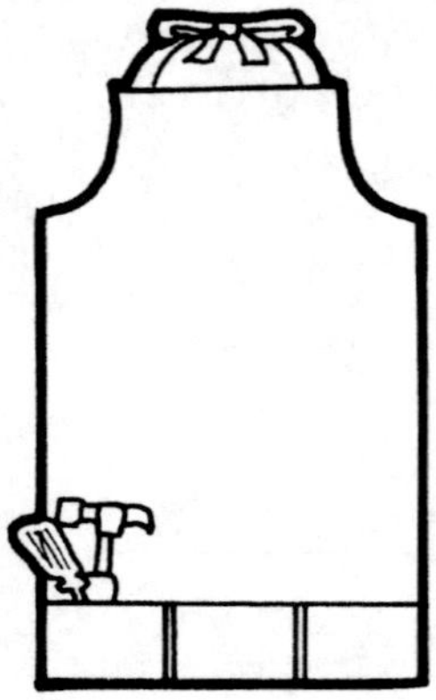

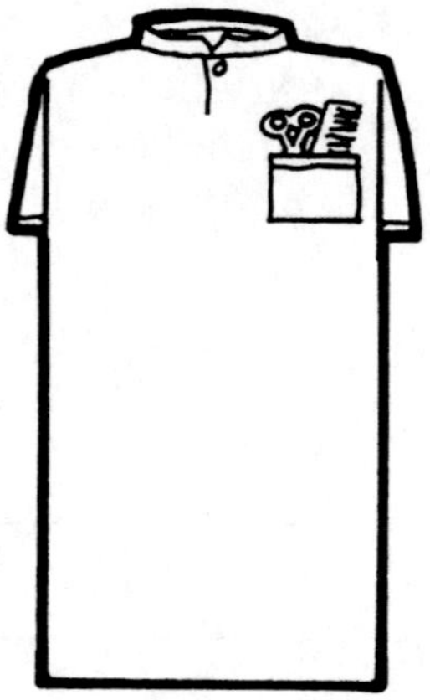

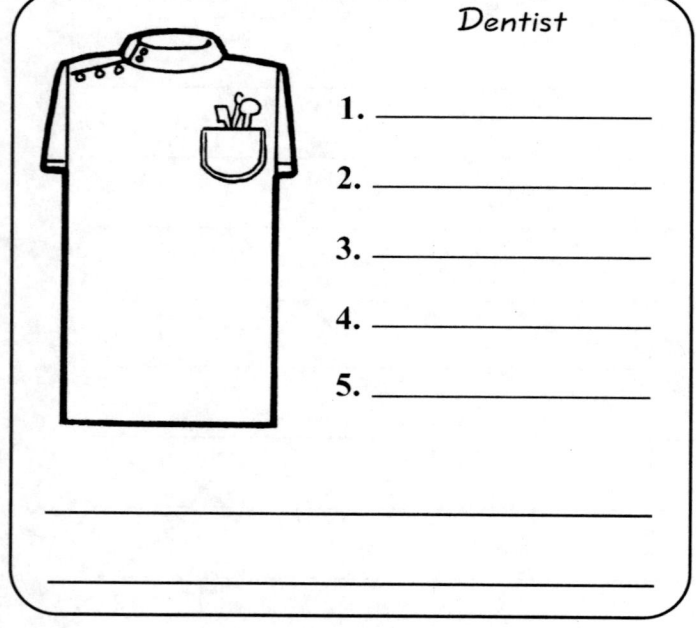

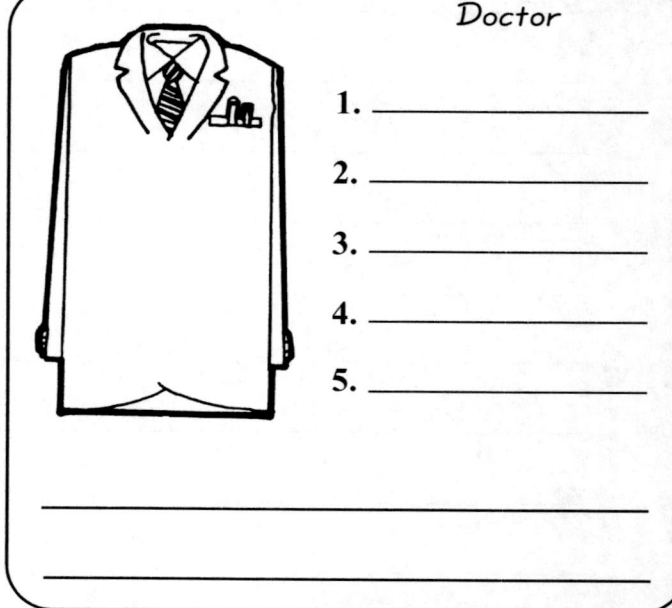

# THE CARNIVAL

There's just so much to see and do when you go to the carnival!

Make a list of things you would see at a carnival.

_____    _____    _____

Make a list of things you would hear at a carnival.

_____    _____    _____

Make a list of things you would smell at a carnival.

_____    _____    _____

Using your word lists, write two paragraphs telling someone about a trip to the carnival!

# GARDENS

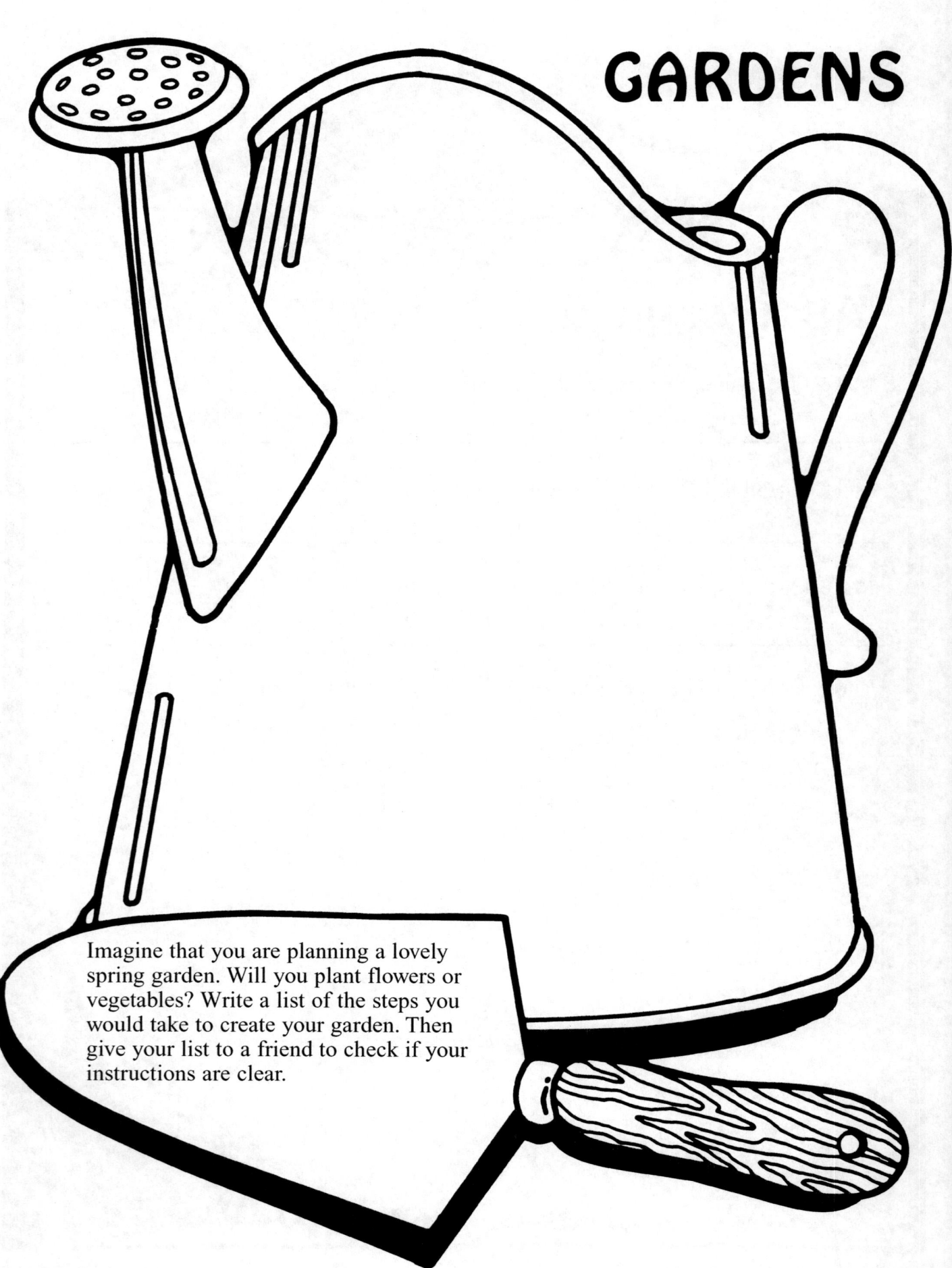

Imagine that you are planning a lovely spring garden. Will you plant flowers or vegetables? Write a list of the steps you would take to create your garden. Then give your list to a friend to check if your instructions are clear.

What kind of tree would you like to have in your yard? Why did you choose that tree?
_____
_____
_____

Describe the tree.
_____
_____
_____
_____

Pretend you are the tree. Look around you. What do you see?
_____
_____
_____

Tell about a way that a tree can be helpful to people or animals.
_____
_____
_____
_____

# TREES

# Communication, Travel & Government
## Related Studies and Activities

Encourage students to explore individual topics on their own, using the related studies and suggested activities listed below.

**Newspapers**  **Related Studies:** Media • Advertising • Investigative Reporting
**Activity:** Work cooperatively to write and publish a classroom newspaper.

**Elections**  **Related Studies:** Presidents • Political Parties • Voting • Government
**Activity:** Vote on a variety of classroom officers and rules.

**Presidents**  **Related Studies:** President's Day • Elections • Revolutionary & Civil Wars
**Activity:** Compile fact lists for each President (or Prime Minister).

**Liberty Bell**  **Related Studies:** Statue of Liberty • Declaration of Independence
**Activity:** Plan and carry out a Fourth of July freedom parade.

**Stars & Stripes**  **Related Studies:** Flag Day • Patriotism • Veterans • State Flags
**Activity:** Design a new flag, based on the elements of the national flag.

**Transportation**  **Related Studies:** Airplanes, Boats & Trains • Inventions • Travel
**Activity:** Using recycled products, invent a unique form of transportation.

**Summer Vacation**  **Related Studies:** Travel • Sports • Weather • Sun • Maps & Globes
**Activity:** Design a poster that illustrates the activities you plan to do during summer vacation.

# NEWSPAPERS

### IN MY OPINION
What job would you like to do at a newspaper? Why?

### HELP WANTED
Write an ad for a job at the newspaper. What would you need to know to do this job?

### READ ALL ABOUT IT!
Name some events that might be written about in a newspaper.

### HOT OFF THE PRESS…
Write a short article about something good that happened at school.

*Fun with Paragraph Writing* © EDUPRESS, INC. EP164

# ELECTIONS

Which of your classmates would make the perfect class president? Make your choice, and then prepare a campaign flyer for your candidate.

What are the qualities needed for a good class president?

Write a paragraph describing the qualities your candidate has that would make him or her a good president.

Write three campaign slogans encouraging voters to vote for your candidate. Circle your favorite slogan.

*Fun with Paragraph Writing*

# Presidents

## A Presidential Profile

A profile of a person lets us learn about him or her. Gather information from the encyclopedia or other resources to write a profile of your favorite US President.

**Information about his life:**

_____
_____
_____
_____

**His most admirable qualities:**

_____
_____
_____
_____

**Contributions and ways he changed people's lives:**

_____
_____
_____
_____

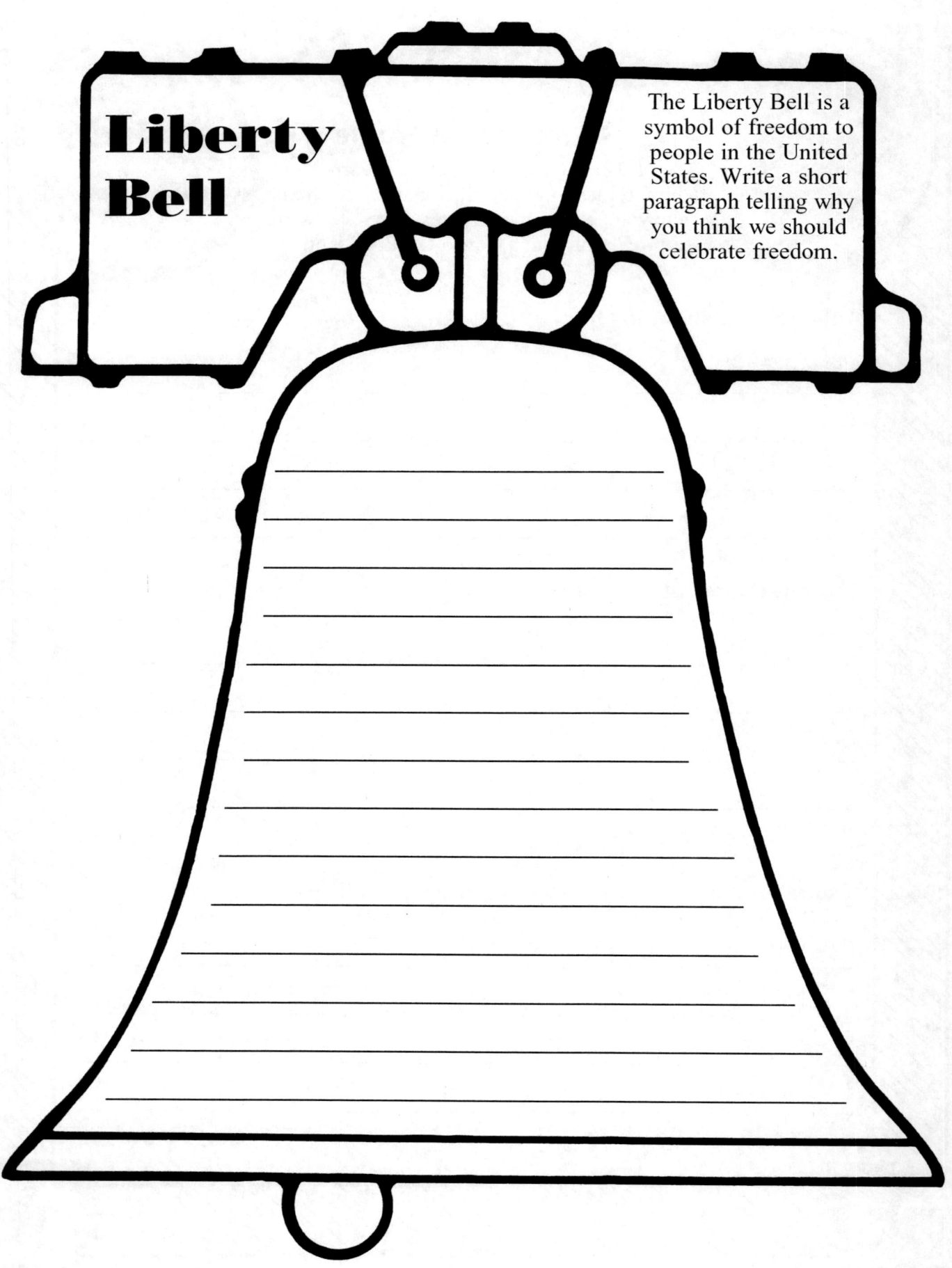

# Stars & Stripes

The flag that symbolizes the United States is sometimes called the Stars & Stripes. Write at least two paragraphs explaining how the colors and design of the flag represent our country.

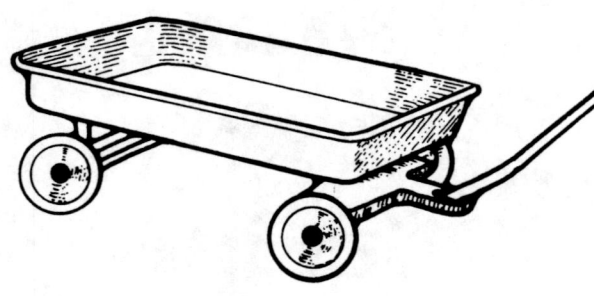

# TRANSPORTATION

Have you ever thought about how many forms of transportation there are for moving people and things? Next to the numbers below, name ten kinds of vehicles. Then on the lines next to your choices, list at least three things that might be transported in each vehicle.

1. _____  _____
2. _____  _____
3. _____  _____
4. _____  _____
5. _____  _____
6. _____  _____
7. _____  _____
8. _____  _____
9. _____  _____
10. _____  _____

What is your favorite kind of transportation? Airplane? Train? Bicycle? Write a paragraph explaining why it is your favorite, and telling about a time when you used that transportation.

# SUMMER VACATION

What is your favorite thing to do for summer vacation? Do you like to go fishing? To the beach? Camping? Write a paragraph describing your ideal summer vacation.

_____
_____
_____
_____
_____
_____

Show your paragraph to a classmate and ask him or her to point out any mistakes or editing changes that you might make. After looking at the comments, write a revised paragraph.

_____
_____
_____
_____
_____
_____

*Fun with Paragraph Writing*

# Understanding Others
## Related Studies and Activities

Encourage students to explore individual topics on their own, using the related studies and suggested activities listed below.

**Family Life**	**Related Studies:** Adoption • Siblings • Family Trees • Grandparents
**Activity:** Make a bulletin board of students' family pictures.

**Mother**	**Related Studies:** Values • Occupations • Generations • Love • Respect
**Activity:** Publish a book of poems about mothers, written by students.

**Father**	**Related Studies:** Neighbors • Apartment Houses • Country Living
**Activity:** Write a poem about a dad—yours or one you admire—to display on a backing of old ties.

**Friends**	**Related Studies:** Sharing • Moving • Responsibility • Family Life
**Activity:** Develop a new friendship with a "secret pal" in class.

**Disabilities**	**Related Studies:** Five Senses • Feelings • Birth Defects
**Activity:** Experiment with a blindfold, ear plugs, and a wheelchair to experience disabilities.

**Draw a family web in the box below, showing all the people in your family and how they are related to one another. Who is at the center of the web?**

Write a short paragraph telling how the people in your family are alike.

Write a short paragraph telling how the people in your family are different.

# Family Life

Mother

If you could share five things with your mother that told her what you thought about her, what would they be?

1. _____
_____
_____
2. _____
_____
_____
3. _____
_____
_____
4. _____
_____
_____
5. _____
_____

Fun with Paragraph Writing

# FATHER

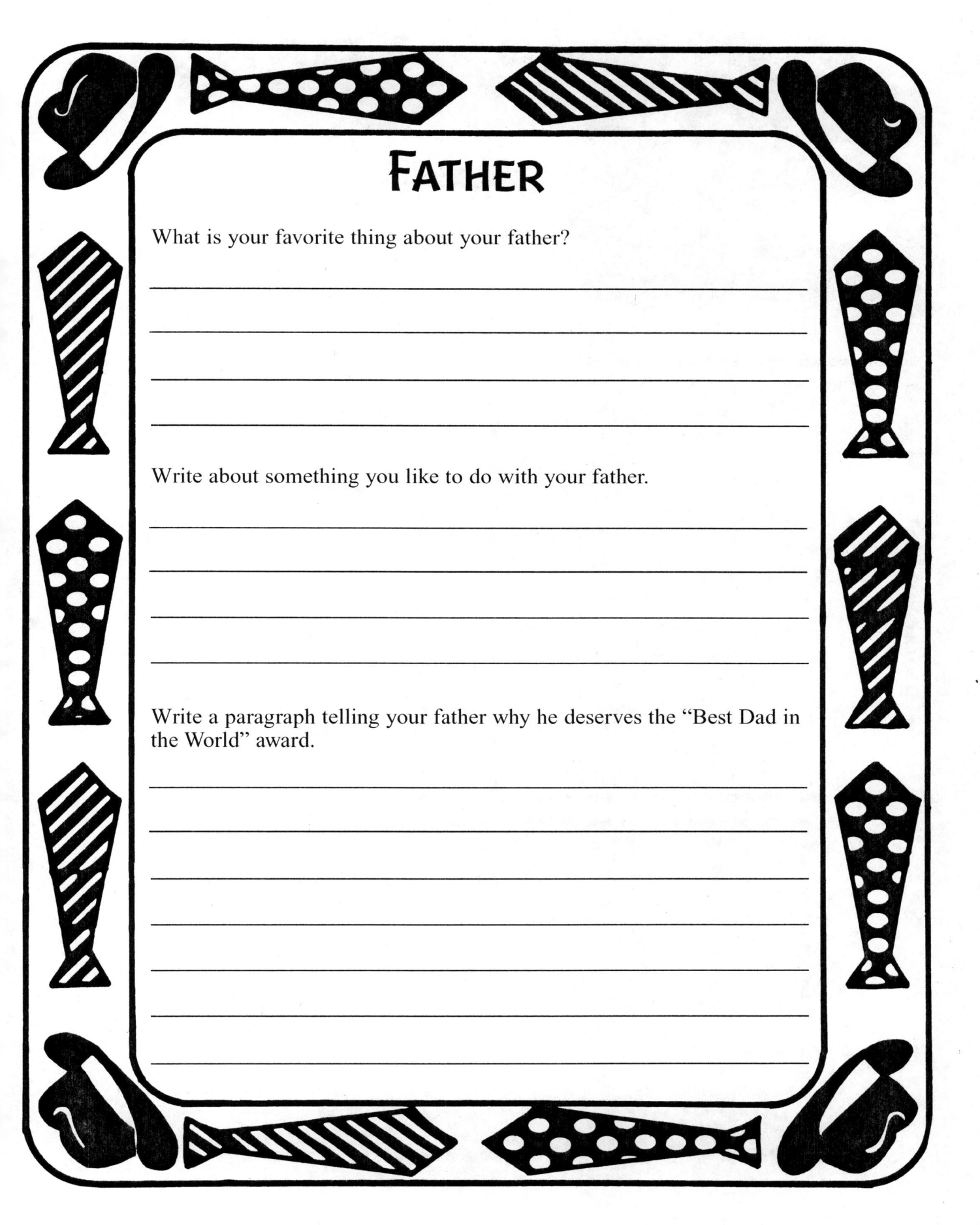

What is your favorite thing about your father?

_____
_____
_____
_____

Write about something you like to do with your father.

_____
_____
_____
_____

Write a paragraph telling your father why he deserves the "Best Dad in the World" award.

_____
_____
_____
_____
_____
_____
_____

# Friends

Write a description of your best friend.

Write about a time when you and your friend had a disagreement.

How was the disagreement between you resolved?

What qualities do you think are most important in a friend?

# Disabilities

There are many people with disabilities who have accomplished important things. As a group, think of some of those people and write their names here.

Select one of the people on your list and write a paragraph about this person's accomplishments.

# History
## Related Studies and Activities

Encourage students to explore individual topics on their own, using the related studies and suggested activities listed below.

**Kings & Queens**
**Related Studies:** Prince • Princess • Castles • Kingdoms • Knights
**Activity:** Assign one student to be king or queen for the day, allowing them to make three rules for the classroom kingdom.

**Castles & Knights**
**Related Studies:** Dragons • Armor • Chivalry • Medieval Times
**Activity:** Divide into cooperative groups to build castle replicas from recycled materials.

**Ancient Egypt**
**Related Studies:** Mummies • Hieroglyphics • Pharaohs • Archaeology
**Activity:** Make a variety of artifacts that might be found in an archaeologic dig in Egypt.

**Native American Legends**
**Related Studies:** Folklore • Tribes • Frontier • Legends • Ceremonies
**Activity:** Study different Native American tribes and create a mural depicting each one's way of life.

**Explorers**
**Related Studies:** Vikings • Maps • Compass • Survival • Heroes
**Activity:** Make a shadow box depicting an explorer and his expedition.

**Coming to a New Land**
**Related Studies:** Colonial Life • Native Americans • Mayflower
**Activity:** Plan a cooking day and recreate recipes based on food early settlers might have raised.

**Pioneers**
**Related Studies:** Native Americans • Wagon Trains • Explorers
**Activity:** Make a cooperative mural that traces and describes the westward trails.

**Cowboys**
**Related Studies:** Frontier Life • Tall Tales • Ranches • Railroads
**Activity:** Plan a reading rodeo—round up books and resources about cowboy life for a class library.

**Martin Luther King, Jr.**
**Related Studies:** African Americans • Civil Rights Movement
**Activity:** Create a time line of the life of another African American.

**African Americans**
**Related Studies:** Slavery • Civil War • Freedom • African Crafts
**Activity:** Select a famous African American and write a poem about him or her.

*Fun with Paragraph Writing*

# KINGS & QUEENS

Imagine that you are a king or a queen. Describe the country over which you govern.

What would a typical day be like for a king or queen? Write a schedule outlining your day.

Write three laws that you think would make the lives of your subjects better.

# CASTLES & KNIGHTS

## A DAY IN THE LIFE OF ...
Choose either knight or castle to complete this story title.
Write a story to go with the title you have chosen.

Name five things that you might see if you lived in Egypt long ago.

Choose one of these things and write a description of it.

Use your description as part of a story about life in ancient Egypt.

*Fun with Paragraph Writing*     31     © EDUPRESS, INC.™     EP164

# Native American Legends

Read a legend told by the Native American tribe of your choice. Write the names of the main characters here.

Now retell the legend in your own words. Read your legend aloud to the rest of the class.

_____
_____
_____
_____
_____
_____
_____
_____
_____
_____
_____
_____
_____
_____
_____
_____
_____
_____

What words would describe the life of an explorer? Exciting? Dangerous? Write a daily journal based on the experiences of an explorer. Circle all of the descriptive words you use.

# EXPLORERS

**Day 1**

**Day 2**

**Day 3**

*Fun with Paragraph Writing*

# Coming to a New Land

Imagine what it would have been like to have been one of the first settlers to reach the shores of New England. What kinds of problems would you have faced? How would you have felt?

Write a paragraph about each of the topics below. Discuss your answers with your classmates.

| What did the new land look like? | What might have been frightening to the new settlers? |
|---|---|
| What daily tasks would you have had to perform? | What would have been the hardest part of living in a new land? |

# PIONEERS

Pretend you are a pioneer crossing the prairie in the 1800s. Write four entries for a diary you are keeping about the daily events in your life.

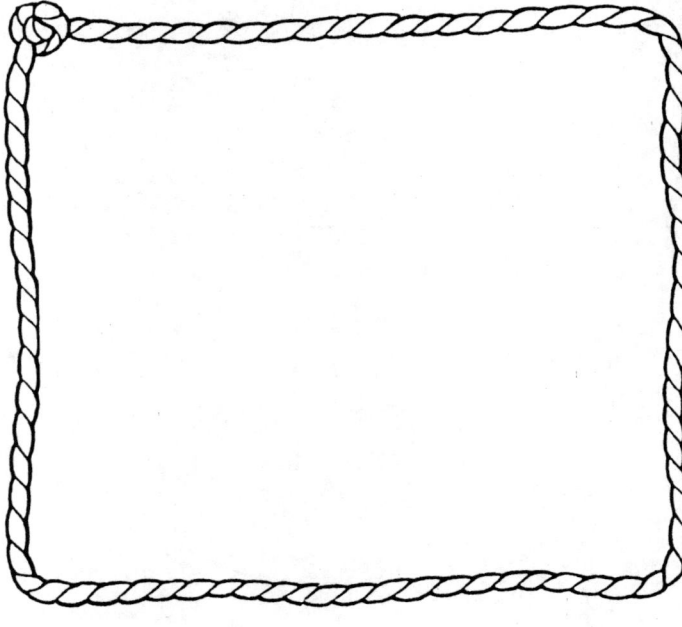
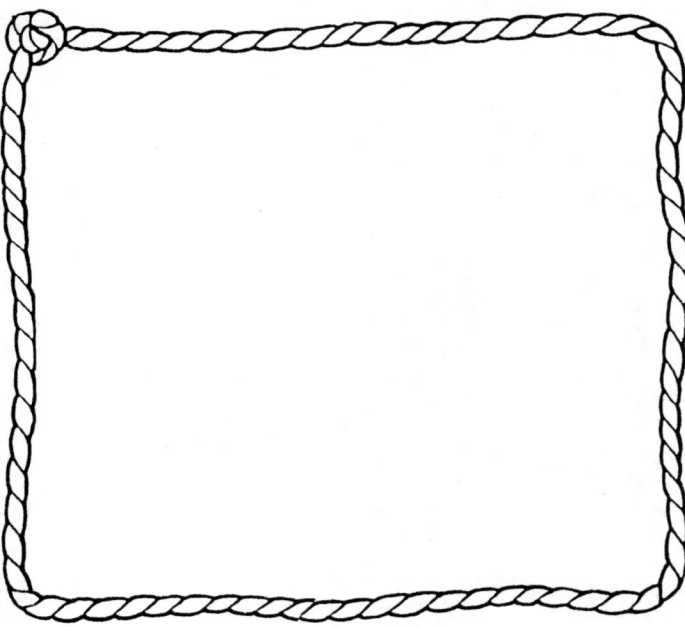
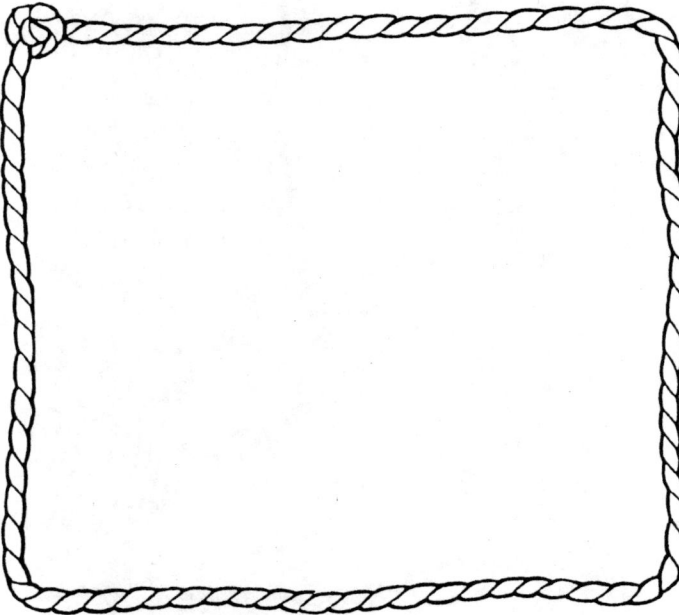

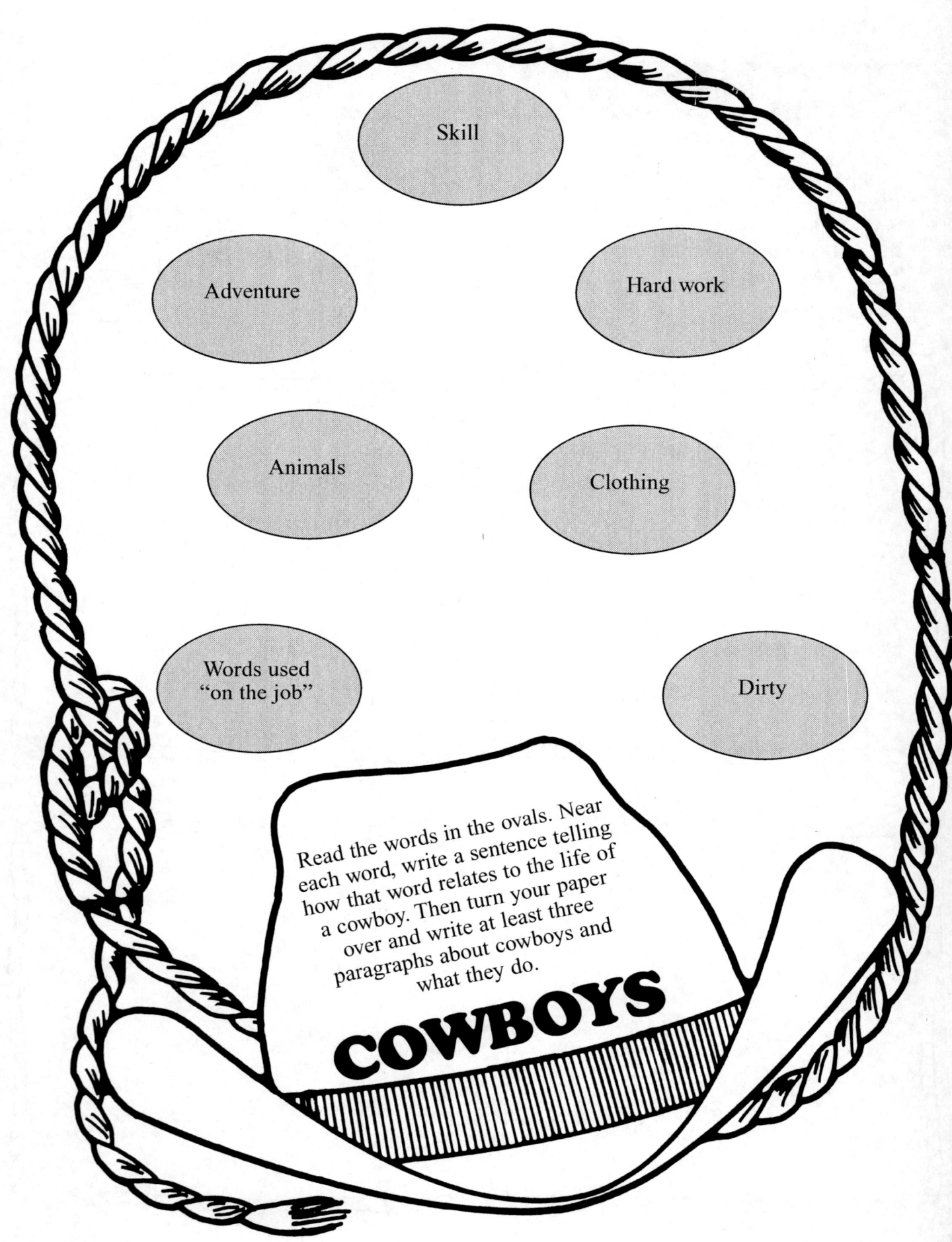

# MARTIN LUTHER KING, JR.

Martin Luther King, Jr. was one of the foremost leaders of the United States' civil rights movement in the 1960s.

Create a time line of some of the major events of his life. Be sure the events are written in the order in which they happened, beginning with number one (1). Write a short paragraph about each event.

**1. Date**

| Event |
|---|

**2. Date**

| Event |
|---|

**3. Date**

| Event |
|---|

**4. Date**

| Event |
|---|

**5. Date**

| Event |
|---|

**6. Date**

| Event |
|---|

*Fun with Paragraph Writing*      © EDUPRESS, INC.™    EP164

# AFRICAN AMERICANS

Read about a noteworthy African American. Think about how this person lived, what kinds of obstacles he or she overcame, and how this person caused changes in the world. Look at each of the words below and write a paragraph about how each word applies to the person you chose.

## FAMILY

## COURAGE

## HERITAGE

## CHANGE

# Countries & Cultures
## Related Studies and Activities

Encourage students to explore individual topics on their own, using the related studies and suggested activities listed below.

**Travel**  
**Related Studies:** Vacations • Maps & Globes • Transportation  
**Activity:** Write a report about a travel destination and put it inside a paper suitcase.

**Foreign Food**  
**Related Studies:** Cooking • Ethnic Differences • Traditions • Holidays  
**Activity:** Find a favorite international food recipe and prepare it in class.

**United States**  
**Related Studies:** Geography • Maps • Population • Regional Differences  
**Activity:** Go on a library "treasure hunt" to look for books about states.

**Canada**  
**Related Studies:** Neighbors • Geography • Provinces • Explorers • Flags  
**Activity:** Divide into cooperative groups to find out about Canada's provinces.

**Eskimos**  
**Related Studies:** Alaska • Temperature • Igloos • Whales • Survival  
**Activity:** Compare the clothes that Eskimos wear to those worn in your daily life.

**Africa**  
**Related Studies:** Tribes • Language • Folklore • Animals  
**Activity:** Make a puppet show that represents some aspect of African culture and present it to another class.

**Mexico**  
**Related Studies:** Aztecs • Civilizations • Volcanoes • Pyramids  
**Activity:** Make a piñata with a paper bag, tissue, and construction paper.

**Japan**  
**Related Studies:** Fairs • Parades • Animals • Lifestyles  
**Activity:** Create Japanese picture scrolls depicting an aspect of the country's culture.

*Fun with Paragraph Writing*

# TRAVEL

Whether it's across the street, across the city, or across the world, it's always exciting to travel to someplace new! Choose your destination and let's plan a trip!

**I would like to go to ...**

**I want to go there because ...**

**Here's what I will pack.**

**How will I get there?**

**When I'm there, I want to see:**

*Fun with Paragraph Writing*

You don't have to travel around the world to taste foreign food. Some of the foods that we eat every day originally came from another country!

Make a list of foods you like that originally came from other countries.

_____
_____
_____

Which is your favorite? Why? What country did it come from?

_____
_____
_____

If you were going to make this, what ingredients would you buy?

_____
_____
_____

Write directions to tell someone how to prepare this food.

_____
_____
_____
_____

*Fun with Paragraph Writing*

# United States

Think about the state in which you live. How would you describe it to someone who had never been there? Can you tell about it in a way that would make them want to move there?

Write a list of words that describe your state: the land, the weather, the people, and things to do.

_____   _____   _____

_____   _____   _____

_____   _____   _____

_____   _____   _____

Now use your list of words to write a travel advertisement for the state you live in, telling the world why it is such a special place.

# Canada

Find and write one interesting fact about Canada's land.

Find and write one interesting fact about Canada's people.

Find and write one more interesting fact about Canada.

Use your facts to write three paragraphs about Canada.

_____
_____
_____
_____
_____
_____
_____
_____
_____
_____
_____
_____
_____
_____

# ESKIMOS

The Eskimos, or *Inuit*, live in the far northern part of the world, where the climate is harsh and often very cold. Think about living in such a climate, and write a paragraph describing a problem an Eskimo might face.

# Africa

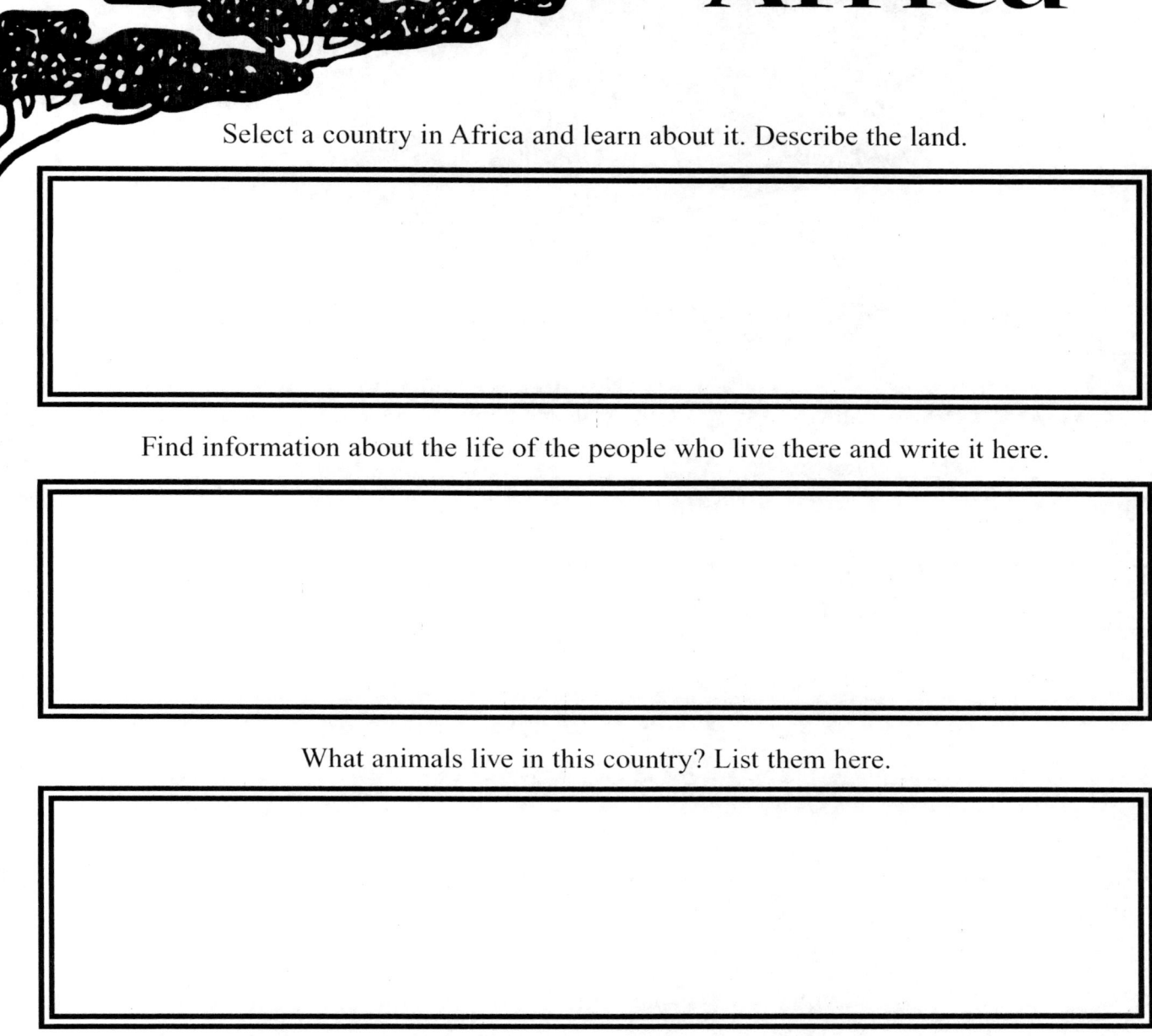

Select a country in Africa and learn about it. Describe the land.

Find information about the life of the people who live there and write it here.

What animals live in this country? List them here.

Use the information you have gathered to write a short report about the country you have chosen.

Would you like to visit this country? How would you get there? Do you think that life there would be very different from where you live? Answer these questions in your report.

Fun with Paragraph Writing   45   © EDUPRESS, INC.™   EP164

# MEXICO

You've just won a trip to Mexico! Where will you visit? What will you see? What will you eat?

Next to the numbers below, write three things you would like to learn about Mexico before you go. Then do some research, writing the information you find in the boxes.

1.

2.

3.

# JAPAN

Imagine you have a Japanese pen pal. Explain how your life in each category below is the same or different compared to life in Japan.

Hobbies:

School:

Food:

Home Life:

*Fun with Paragraph Writing*  47  © EDUPRESS, INC.™  EP164

# Seasons, Holidays & Traditions
## Related Studies and Activities

Encourage students to explore individual topics on their own, using the related studies and suggested activities listed below.

**Snow!**
**Related Studies:** Temperature • Winter • Storms • Seasons
**Activity:** Make a list of the consequences of a snow storm.

**Fall Fun**
**Related Studies:** Leaves • Sports • School • Halloween • Harvest
**Activity:** Plan and carry out a cooperative project appropriate to a fall day.

**Birthdays!**
**Related Studies:** Age • Family Trees • Traditions • Baking • Calendars
**Activity:** Start a birthday tradition to honor each class member.

**Presents**
**Related Studies:** Values • Friendship • Traditions • Birthdays • Customs
**Activity:** Learn how to measure wrapping paper and wrap a gift box.

**Pumpkins**
**Related Studies:** Halloween Customs • Gardens • Shapes • Vines
**Activity:** Draw a jack-o'-lantern face using only geometric shapes.

**Ghost Story**
**Related Studies:** Halloween • Costumes • Haunted Houses • Legends
**Activity:** Write about a Halloween legend.

**Turkey and Trimmings**
**Related Studies:** Family • Harvest • Pilgrims • Native Americans
**Activity:** Graph the traditional food items that students have for Thanksgiving dinner.

**Hanukkah**
**Related Studies:** Dreidel • Jewish Holidays • Latkes • Customs
**Activity:** Write about eight special gifts you have received in your life.

**Christmas Traditions**
**Related Studies:** Global Awareness • Multiculturalism • Sharing
**Activity:** Make a Venn Diagram of the similarities and differences of students' holiday traditions.

**Santa Claus**
**Related Studies:** North Pole • Christmas around the World
**Activity:** Write a tale about how Santa Claus got his suit.

**Reindeer**
**Related Studies:** Arctic Animals • Antarctica • Hibernation
**Activity:** Make a puppet of an Arctic animal and present a short skit.

**Chinese New Year**
**Related Studies:** Dragons • Multiculturalism • Folklore
**Activity:** Paint a dragon based on a cooperatively created description.

**Groundhog Day**
**Related Studies:** Hibernation • Animal in Winter • Shadows • Spring
**Activity:** Make a chart of hibernating animals.

**My Valentine**
**Related Studies:** Pen Pals • Letter Writing • Friendship • Values
**Activity:** Write one letter each week to a classmate.

**Leprechauns**
**Related Studies:** Ireland • St. Patrick's Day • Superstition
**Activity:** Plan a reader's theater to celebrate St. Patrick's Day.

**Bunnies**
**Related Studies:** Easter • Pets • Traditions • Animal Life
**Activity:** Invite a pet store owner to visit class and bring a bunny to share.

*Fun with Paragraph Writing*

# Snow!

Imagine that you are a snowman. Tell the story of the day you were created!

# Fall Fun

In the first box below, brainstorm a list of words that describe fall. In the next two boxes, use your list of words to write paragraphs about fall weather and your favorite fall activities.

**Fall Words**

**Fall Weather**

**Fall Activities**

# BIRTHDAYS!

Pretend a friend gave you a surprise birthday party. Write a letter to thank your friend, mentioning the decorations, what you ate, the presents you received, and the good time you had.

Dear

Your Friend,

*Fun with Paragraph Writing*

# Presents

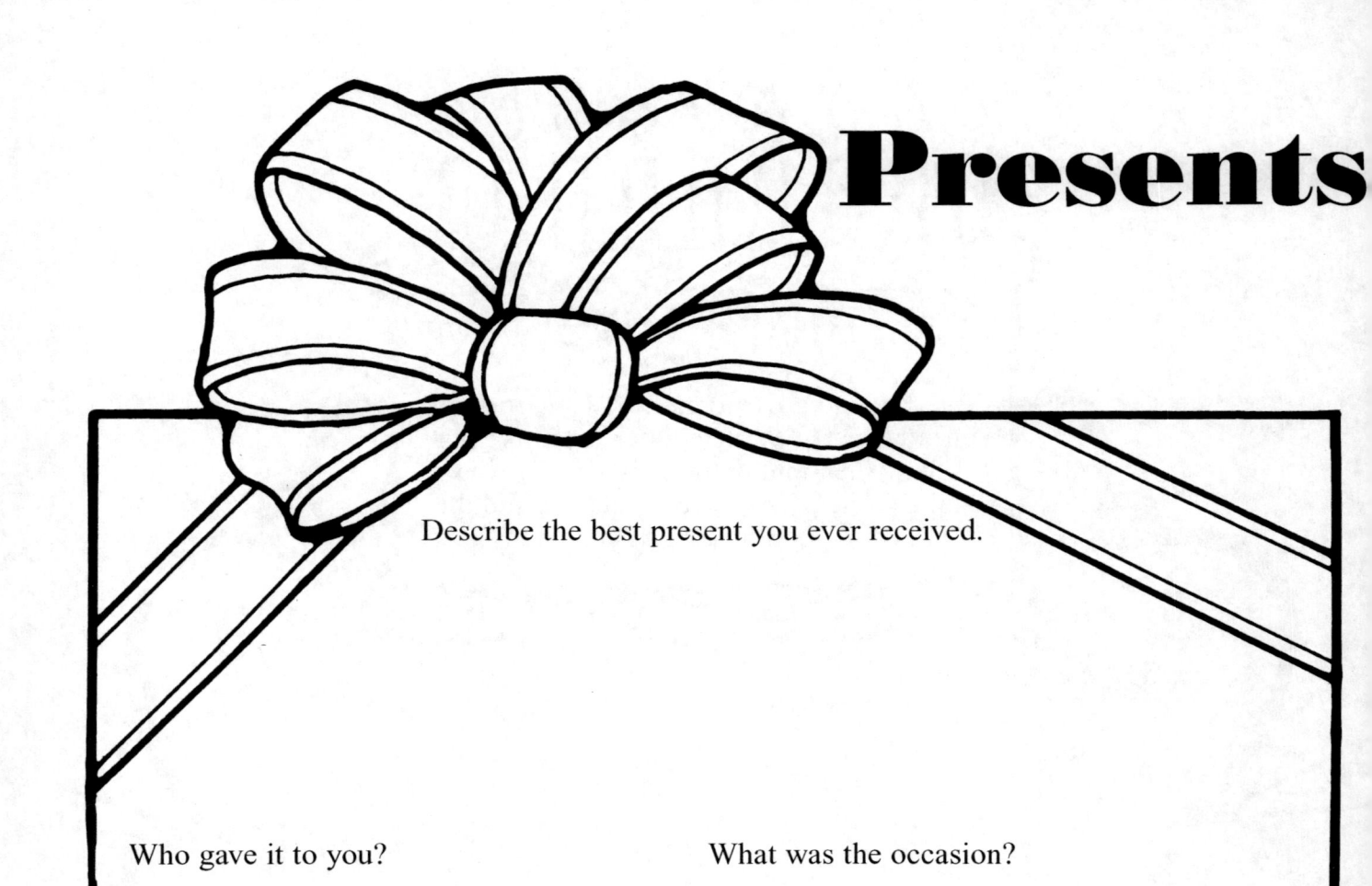

Describe the best present you ever received.

Who gave it to you?   What was the occasion?

Write a paragraph explaining why this present was so special.

# PUMPKINS

Write at least three sentences describing a pumpkin.

Name at least three uses for a pumpkin.

What is your favorite thing to do with a pumpkin? Write a paragraph telling how you like to use a pumpkin.

# GHOST STORY

Make a "ghost" acrostic by writing five sentences about ghosts. Begin each sentence with a letter from the word GHOST. Using the sentences as a beginning, write a ghost story and read it to your classmates.

**G** _____
**H** _____
**O** _____
**S** _____
**T** _____

_____
_____
_____
_____
_____
_____
_____
_____
_____
_____
_____
_____

*Fun with Paragraph Writing*

# Turkey and Trimmings

In each of the boxes below, write the name of one of your favorite Thanksgiving foods. Under each food, write a paragraph to describe it.

# Hanukkah

Do some research about Hanukkah.

Write paragraphs about eight facts or traditions that you learned about the holiday.

| | |
|---|---|
| 1. | 2. |
| 3. | 4. |
| 5. | 6. |
| 7. | 8. |

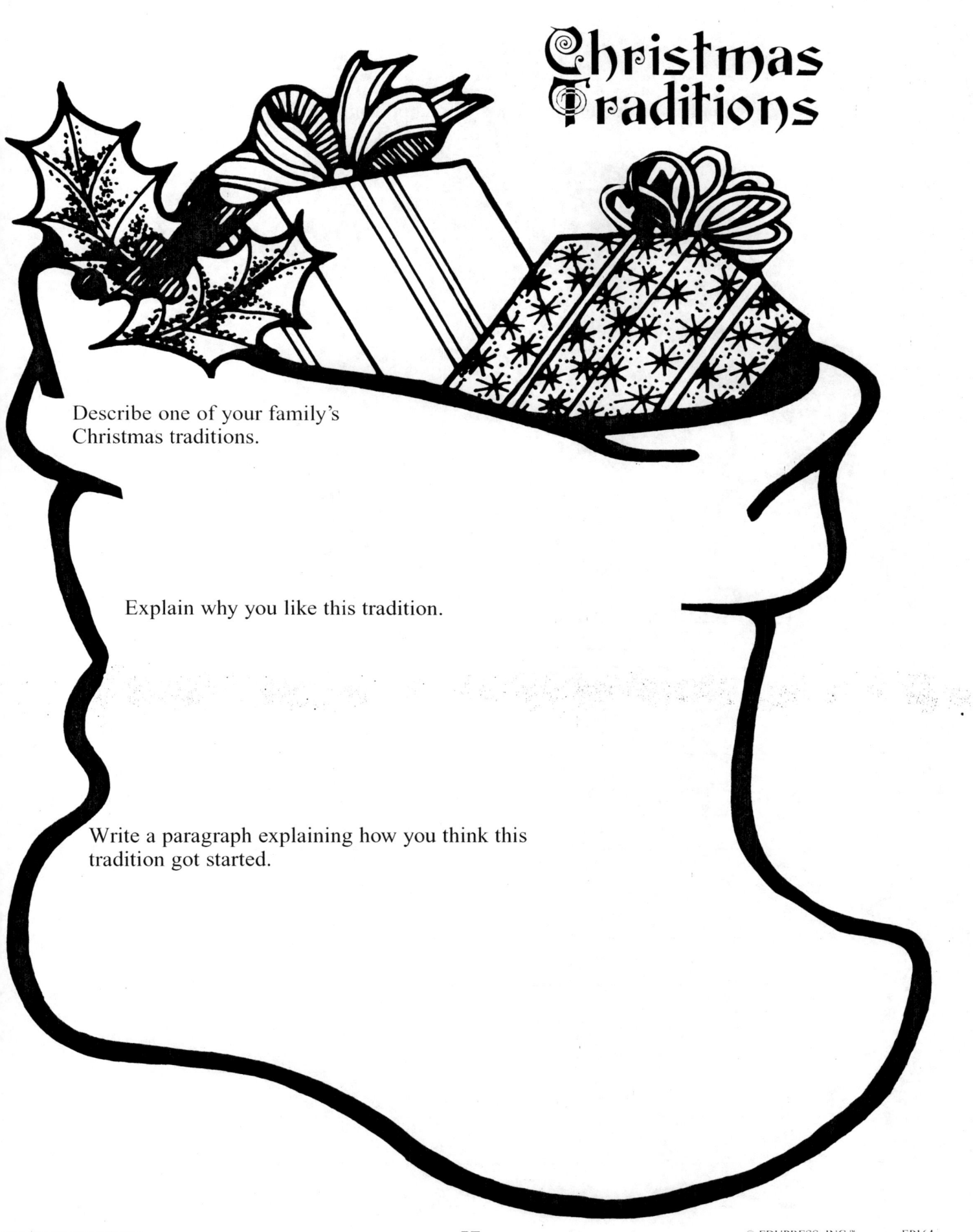

# Christmas Traditions

Describe one of your family's Christmas traditions.

Explain why you like this tradition.

Write a paragraph explaining how you think this tradition got started.

*Fun with Paragraph Writing*

# Santa Claus

Santa has decided to move his workshop from the North Pole to Hawaii. Write a story of Santa on the beach.

# Reindeer & Other Arctic Animals

**Wanted:**
Animal to guide a sleigh on Christmas Eve. Must be strong, dependable, and willing to travel. Send application to Santa Claus, Box 1225, North Pole

Describe the animal you think will answer the ad. Do you think the animal fits the qualifications? Why?

Write a paragraph describing the animal's first night "on the job."

# Chinese New Year

Write a list of words that describe a
Chinese New Year celebration:

_____

_____

_____

_____

_____

_____

_____

Use the words from your list to write at least two paragraphs telling about the Chinese New Year.

_____

_____

_____

_____

_____

_____

_____

_____

_____

_____

_____

_____

_____

# Groundhog Day

Tradition says that when the groundhog pokes his head out of the ground on Groundhog Day, he is looking for his shadow. If he sees his shadow, it means that there will be six more weeks of winter. If there is no shadow to be seen, spring is just around the corner.

| Write a paragraph explaining how you think the tradition of Groundhog Day began. | Do you think the tradition is true? Write a paragraph explaining why or why not. |
|---|---|
| | |

# My Valentine

What would you do on Valentine's Day to show someone that you care about him or her? Make a list of the things you can think of. Then write a paragraph to your valentine explaining why you think he or she is so special.

_____          _____

_____          _____

_____          _____

_____          _____

_____          _____

# Leprechauns

List four words that describe leprechauns.

_____
_____
_____
_____

Describe something that you've heard a leprechaun can do.

_____
_____
_____
_____

Do you believe leprechauns are real? Write a paragraph explaining why or why not.

_____
_____
_____
_____
_____
_____
_____
_____

# BUNNIES

Nothing says spring like a bunny! Write about what your day would be like if you were a bunny!

| Write a paragraph about what you would eat. | Write a paragraph about where you would live. |
| --- | --- |
| Write a paragraph about your favorite things to do. | Write a paragraph about your friends. |